Deuteronomy 28
A key
to understanding

I0164314

Michael Penny

ISBN: 978-1-78364-467-4

www.obt.org.uk

****

The Open Bible Trust
Fordland Mount, Upper Basildon,
Reading, RG8 8LU, UK.

Deuteronomy 28
A key to understanding

Contents

Page

5   Introduction

7   The Law of Moses

8   Food, clothing and health

9   Protection from enemies

9   A special Nation

11   No food and no clothes

11   No protection from enemies

12   Not a special nation

15   The Judges

23   The Kings

33   The Prophets

39   Judgment fell

47   The New Testament

51   The sin of ignorance

53   The Messiah in the Old Testament

64   The Judgment and then Acts 28

67   Appendix 1: What happened after the end
          of Acts?

73   The change

81   Appendix 2: Deuteronomy 28 and Josephus

85   Appendix 3: The New Covenant

86   About the Author

91   Also by Michael Penny

93   Free Magazine

94   About this book

Introduction

Deuteronomy 28 is a chapter which is seldom referred to in commentaries and Christian literature, yet it is fundamental to understanding how God was dealing with the Nation of Israel in the rest of the Old Testament. Not only that, it helps us understand some of the things Christ said to the Jews and some of the events which happened to their nation in the first century AD.

Following Israel's exodus from Egypt, they entered the wilderness where God spoke to Moses. He was given the terms of a covenant (or contract) between God and the Nation of Israel. The terms of this covenant, often referred to as the Old Covenant, were as follows:

> "This is what you are to say to the house of Jacob and what you are to tell the people of Israel: 'You yourselves have seen what I did to Egypt, and how I carried you on eagles' wings and brought you to myself. Now if you obey me fully and keep my

covenant, then out of all nations you will be my treasured possession. Although the whole earth is mine, you will be for me a kingdom of priests and a holy nation.' These are the words you are to speak to the Israelites."

So Moses went back and summoned the elders of the people and set before them all the words the LORD had commanded him to speak. The people all responded together, "We will do everything the LORD has said." So Moses brought their answer back to the LORD. (Exodus 19:3-8)

The Nation of Israel agreed that they would fully obey God and keep what was to become known as the Law of Moses. If they did so, then they would become a kingdom of priests, a holy nation, and a treasured possession. But was God expecting 100% compliance? One suspects not, for if anyone had managed to fully obey, for all of the time, then that person would never have sinned and would have been perfect, requiring neither forgiveness nor a Saviour.

The Law of Moses

Deuteronomy is the second giving of the Law and has some additional items to both Exodus and Leviticus. Deuteronomy 28 builds upon Exodus 19 and expands it. There we read:

> If you fully obey the LORD your God and carefully follow all his commands that I give you today, the LORD your God will set you high above all the nations on earth. All these blessings will come upon you and accompany you if you obey the LORD your God. (Deuteronomy 28:1-2)

Here, again, is the need to fully obey, and here again is the promise that Israel will be the premier nation on earth. However, verses 3-13 goes on to mention certain blessings that would come upon the Nation of Israel if they did fully obey. If we look at these closely we see that they fall roughly into three categories:

Food, clothing and health

You will be blessed in the city and blessed in the country. The fruit of your womb will be blessed, and the crops of your land and the young of your livestock—the calves of your herds and the lambs of your flocks. Your basket and your kneading trough will be blessed. You will be blessed when you come in and blessed when you go out ... The LORD will send a blessing on your barns and on everything you put your hand to. The LORD your God will bless you in the land he is giving you. (vs 3-6,8)

The LORD will grant you abundant prosperity—in the fruit of your womb, the young of your livestock and the crops of your ground—in the land he swore to your forefathers to give you. The LORD will open the heavens, the storehouse of his bounty, to send rain on your land in season and to bless all the work of your hands. You will lend to many nations but will borrow from none. (vs 11-12)

Protection from enemies

The LORD will grant that the enemies who rise up against you will be defeated before you. They will come at you from one direction but flee from you in seven. (v 7)

A special Nation

The LORD will establish you as his holy people, as he promised you on oath, if you keep the commands of the LORD your God and walk in his ways. Then all the peoples on earth will see that you are called by the name of the LORD, and they will fear you. (vs 9-10)

The LORD will make you the head, not the tail. If you pay attention to the commands of the LORD your God that I give you this day and carefully follow them, you will always be at the top, never at the bottom. (v 13)

And Moses finishes this section on blessings with the exhortation:

> Do not turn aside from any of the commands I give you today, to the right or to the left, following other gods and serving them. (v 14)

This emphasis on agricultural blessing may surprise us, but it should not. Many countries today struggle to provide sufficient food for their population and in Old Testament (and New Testament) times this was even more of a difficulty. To have reliable harvests and good flocks and herds, providing both food and clothing, would go a long way to ensuring they would be a healthy and happy Nation.

But what would happen if they disobeyed? The next section of Deuteronomy 28 deals with that.

> However, if you do not obey the LORD your God and do not carefully follow all his commands and decrees I am giving you

today, all these curses will come upon you and overtake you. (v 15)

And if we read the list of curses (judgments) that were to befall the Nation of Israel they, again, fall roughly into the same three categories. We will not quote all the judgments but they include:

No food and no clothes

You will be cursed in the city and cursed in the country. Your basket and your kneading trough will be cursed. The fruit of your womb will be cursed, and the crops of your land, and the calves of your herds and the lambs of your flocks. (vs 16-18)

No protection from enemies

The LORD will cause you to be defeated before your enemies. You will come at them from one direction but flee from them in seven, and you will become a thing of horror to all the kingdoms on earth (v 25)

The LORD will bring a nation against you from far away, from the ends of the earth, like an eagle swooping down, a nation whose language you will not understand, a fierce-looking nation without respect for the old or pity for the young. (vs 49-50)

Then the LORD will scatter you among all nations, from one end of the earth to the other. (v 64)

Not a special nation

The LORD will drive you and the king you set over you to a nation unknown to you or your fathers. There you will worship other gods, gods of wood and stone. You will become a thing of horror and an object of scorn and ridicule to all the nations where the LORD will drive you. (vs 36-37)

The alien who lives among you will rise above you higher and higher, but you will sink lower and lower. He will lend to you, but you will not lend to him. He will be the head, but you will be the tail. (vs 43-44)

This is the justice of the Law of Moses: blessings for obedience, but judgments for disobedience. However, if we return to our earlier question: what level of obedience did God require? It could not have been 100%, or else they would have been perfect, sinless. That being the case, how did Israel know whether or not their compliance was sufficiently high to warrant God's approval? Deuteronomy 28 provides the answer.

All these curses will come upon you. They will pursue you and overtake you until you are destroyed, because you did not obey the LORD your God and observe the commands and decrees he gave you. *They will be a sign* and a wonder to you and your descendants for ever. (vs 45-46)

Thus this system of blessings and judgments was *a sign* to the people of Israel, and as such it guided them. If the nation was being blessed, that was a sign to them that they were meeting God's requirements. On the other hand if they were suffering, it was a sign to them that they were not, and thus they should repent and turn back to God and His ways.

This was a sign and a wonder God gave to the people of Israel and to their descendants, and it should not be applied to the Gentile Christian Church of today. That generation came out of Egypt and wandered in the wilderness and, eventually, settled in the Promised Land. In spite of their failures, as they wandered the Lord fed them with manna and quail, brought water from a rock and their clothes did not wear out (Exodus 16:13,31;17:6; Numbers 11:31; 20:11; Deuteronomy 8:4). In the land they were protected from their enemies and He did, indeed, bless them under the terms of Deuteronomy 28, even though their obedience was not 100%.

The Judges

After the death of Moses, Joshua led the Nation of Israel into the Promised Land and Joshua's generation was also blessed by the Lord. However, the following generation was very different.

> After that whole generation had been gathered to their fathers, another generation grew up, who knew neither the LORD nor what he had done for Israel. Then the Israelites did evil in the eyes of the LORD and served the Baals. They forsook the LORD, the God of their fathers, who had brought them out of Egypt. They followed and worshipped various gods of the peoples around them. They provoked the LORD to anger because they forsook him and served Baal and the Ashtoreths. In his anger against Israel the LORD handed them over to raiders who plundered them. He sold them to their enemies all around, whom they were no longer able to resist.

Whenever Israel went out to fight, the hand of the LORD was against them to defeat them, just as he had sworn to them. They were in great distress. (Judges 2:10-15)

And so the Nation of Israel, at that time, failed. They did not come up to the standard God desired and under the terms of Deuteronomy 28 they were to be judged. However, later in Deuteronomy we read:

When all these blessings and curses I have set before you come upon you and you take them to heart wherever the LORD your God disperses you among the nations, and when you and your children return to the LORD your God and obey him with all your heart and with all your soul according to everything I command you today, then the LORD your God will restore your fortunes and have compassion on you and gather you again from all the nations where he scattered you. (Deuteronomy 30:1-3)

The Lord will judge his people, and have compassion on his servants when he sees their strength is gone and no one is left, slave or free. (Deuteronomy 32:36; see also Psalm 103:6-14)

And so the goodness and kindness, the mercy and compassion, the love and grace, of God often delayed the judgment, curtailed it or put it off altogether. Here in the time of the Judges, it was often curtailed, for we read:

> Then the LORD raised up judges, who saved them out of the hands of these raiders ... Whenever the LORD raised up a judge for them, he was with the judge and saved them out of the hands of their enemies as long as the judge lived; for the LORD had compassion on them as they groaned under those who oppressed and afflicted them. (Judges 2:16,18)

And so the Nation would turn back to God and all would be well with them, and they would receive the blessings of Deuteronomy 28. However,

> When the judge died, the people returned to ways even more corrupt than those of their fathers, following other gods and serving and worshipping them. They refused to give up their evil practices and stubborn ways. Therefore the LORD was very angry with Israel and said, "Because this nation has violated the covenant that I laid down for their forefathers and has not listened to me, I will no longer drive out before them any of the nations Joshua left when he died. I will use them to test Israel and see whether they will keep the way of the Lord and walk in it as their forefathers did." (Judges 2:19-22)

And this, basically, is the story of the period of Judges. Successive periods of obedience and blessings, followed by times of disobedience and judgment. The Judges' role was to lead the people of Israel and administer the Law of

Moses, judging in all matters of dispute. They were God-fearing men.

By and large the Nation of Israel, the ordinary people, followed their leaders. If they had a good, God-honouring leader (like one of the Judges) then the nation would follow the lead given by that person. However, if their leaders were corrupt and put more faith in idols, such as Baal and Ashtoreth, then the ordinary people would be lead astray, and the Nation would enter a time of judgment. Thus the leaders were crucial in all of this.

In fact, in the Law of Moses, the leaders (elders) held a significant position. For example, if the Nation sinned unintentionally, through ignorance of some aspect of the Law of Moses, we read:

> If the whole Israelite community sins unintentionally and does what is forbidden in any of the LORD's commands, even though the community is unaware of the matter, they are guilty. When they become aware of the sin they committed, the

assembly must bring a young bull as a sin offering and present it before the Tent of Meeting. The elders of the community are to lay their hands on the bull's head before the LORD, and the bull shall be slaughtered before the LORD. (Leviticus 4:13-15)

In Britain today, and most other countries, if not all, there is a law stating that ignorance of the Law is no excuse, or defence, for breaking the Law, and equally punishable. This is not dissimilar to the Law of Moses, for even if Israel sinned unintentionally, there still had to be a sacrifice for sin, but it was the leaders who were responsible for making that sacrifice.

It was also the leaders who reported to Moses (Exodus 16:22); they served as judges in minor disputes (Exodus 18:26); they went with Moses and Aaron and saw God (Exodus 24:11); they were there for the dedication of the altar (Numbers 7:84); and the leaders were responsible for the behaviour of their people (Numbers 25:1-5). Thus it was essential that the leaders set a good example by observing God's commands in the Law of Moses.

The last two judges were Eli (1 Samuel 4:18) and Samuel (1 Samuel 7:15-16). However, things were about to change. Samuel wanted his sons to be judges over Israel and administer the Law, but there were problems.

> When Samuel grew old, he appointed his sons as judges for Israel. The name of his firstborn was Joel and the name of his second was Abijah, and they served at Beersheba. But his sons did not walk in his ways. They turned aside after dishonest gain and accepted bribes and perverted justice.
>
> So all the elders of Israel gathered together and came to Samuel at Ramah. They said to him, "You are old, and your sons do not walk in your ways; now appoint a king to lead us, such as all the other nations have." (1 Samuel 8:1-5)

Here again we see the elders being proactive, being concerned that if the main judges in Israel did not follow the ways of the Lord, then the Nation would follow them into disobedience and judgments would follow.

The Kings

The request for a king displeased Samuel, but God had already made provision for this event in the Law of Moses.

When you enter the land the LORD your God is giving you and have taken possession of it and settled in it, and you say, "Let us set a king over us like all the nations around us," be sure to appoint over you the king the LORD your God chooses. He must be from among your own brothers. Do not place a foreigner over you, one who is not a brother Israelite. The king, moreover, must not acquire great numbers of horses for himself or make the people return to Egypt to get more of them, for the LORD has told you, "You are not to go back that way again." He must not take many wives, or his heart will be led astray. He must not accumulate large amounts of silver and gold.

When he takes the throne of his kingdom, he is to write for himself on a scroll a copy of this law, taken from that of the priests, who are Levites. It is to be with him, and he is to read it all the days of his life so that he may learn to revere the LORD his God and follow carefully all the words of this law and these decrees and not consider himself better than his brothers and turn from the law to the right or to the left. Then he and his descendants will reign a long time over his kingdom in Israel. (Deuteronomy 17:14-20)

Here we see that one of the principal duties of the king was to make his own copy of the Law, to write it himself on a scroll. Then he was to read it every day, and carefully follow all its decrees.

If he did this, then the Nation would have a godly leader and, by emulating him, they would, themselves, be obeying God's commandments and all the blessings of Deuteronomy 28 would follow. However, if the king did not follow the Law, then he would lead the people astray, and the judgments would follow. Thus the leader, the king, was crucial.

The first king was Saul, who started off well, but struggled as time went by and, in the end, failed rather badly. Samuel went to him and told him:

> "You acted foolishly ... You have not kept the command the LORD your God gave you; if you had, he would have established your kingdom over Israel for all time. But now your kingdom will not endure; the LORD has sought out a man after his own heart and appointed him leader of his people, because you have not kept the LORD's command." (1 Samuel 13:13-14)

As in the days of the Judges, when God would raise up another judge, He was now to raise a new king, one "after his own heart" (see also Acts 13:22). David was an outstanding king because he was an outstanding believer. God was with Him and, under the terms of Deuteronomy 28, God blessed David and the Nation, so much so, that never before had Israel been so affluent, so powerful, so influential.

However, it is likely that Deuteronomy 28 needs to be understood as a 'national' blessing rather than 'individualistic'. Even in David's day there were still some 'bad' people who prospered while some 'good' people suffered; see, for example Psalm 73 written by Asaph, the choral leader during David's reign. Of course on the personal level there was the 'natural' consequence of following God's commands, for obeying the Law of Moses would naturally lead to healthier lives and better family relationships, as well as an improved society.

David did commit a terrible sin with respect to Bathsheba and her husband Uriah. However, his heartfelt repentance can be seen in Psalm 51, and forgiveness was granted, so much so that a son which David later had by Bathsheba became the next king.

Solomon started off brilliantly, asking for wisdom and using it. Israel's wealth and sphere of influence was even greater than under David, and the temple was built in Jerusalem. But Solomon had a great weakness. Partly due to his political influence over other nations, he ended up with hundreds of wives;

> King Solomon, however, loved many foreign women besides Pharaoh's daughter- -Moabites, Ammonites, Edomites, Sidonians and Hittites. They were from nations about which the LORD had told the Israelites, "You must not intermarry with them, because they will surely turn your hearts after their gods." Nevertheless, Solomon held fast to them in love.
>
> He had seven hundred wives of royal birth and three hundred concubines, and his wives led him astray. As Solomon grew old, his wives turned his heart after other gods, and his heart was not fully devoted to the LORD his God, as the heart of David his father had been. He followed Ashtoreth the goddess of the Sidonians, and Molech the detestable god of the Ammonites.

So Solomon did evil in the eyes of the LORD; he did not follow the LORD completely, as David his father had done. On a hill east of Jerusalem, Solomon built a high place for Chemosh the detestable god of Moab, and for Molech the detestable god of the Ammonites. He did the same for all his foreign wives, who burned incense and offered sacrifices to their gods.

The LORD became angry with Solomon because his heart had turned away from the LORD, the God of Israel, who had appeared to him twice. Although he had forbidden Solomon to follow other gods, Solomon did not keep the LORD's command. So the LORD said to Solomon, "Since this is your attitude and you have not kept my covenant and my decrees, which I commanded you, I will most certainly tear the kingdom away from you and give it to one of your subordinates. Nevertheless, for the sake of David your father, I will not do it during your lifetime. I will tear it out of the hand of your son. Yet I will not tear the whole kingdom from him, but will give him one tribe for the sake of David my servant and for the sake of Jerusalem, which I have chosen." (1 Kings 11:1-13)

The wisest of all men, a man to whom the Lord appeared, became a fool, for he failed to follow the Law of Moses. It clearly stated that the Israelites should not marry into certain nations, and it clearly stated that the king "must not take many wives" and it clearly stated what the consequences would be; "his heart will be led astray" (Deuteronomy 17:17).

If the king built temples for foreign gods and worshipped these idols, and indulged in the pagan practices associated with worship (some of which were not only immoral but also horrific) how many people in the Nation followed suit? Thus judgment under the terms of Deuteronomy 28 was to fall, and it fell in the form of civil war, the result of which that after the death of Solomon the Nation split in two: the northern kingdom of Israel (with ten tribes) and the southern kingdom of Judah (with two tribes).

And this was the continuing story of the Old Testament. There was a succession of kings for both the northern and southern kingdom; some did what was right, and some did what was wrong. For example, we read:

> Nadab son of Jeroboam became king of Israel in the second year of Asa king of Judah, and he reigned over Israel for two years. *He did evil in the eyes of the LORD*, walking in the ways of his father and in his *sin, which he had caused Israel to commit.* (1 Kings 15:25-26)

> In the third year of Asa king of Judah, Baasha son of Ahijah became king of all Israel in Tirzah, and he reigned for twenty-four years. *He did evil in the eyes of the LORD*, walking in the ways of Jeroboam and in his *sin, which he had caused Israel to commit.* (1 Kings 15:33-34)

> But *Omri did evil in the eyes of the LORD* and sinned more than all those before him. He walked in all the ways of Jeroboam son

of Nebat and in his *sin, which he had caused Israel to commit,* so that they provoked the LORD, the God of Israel, to anger by their worthless idols. (1 Kings 16:25-26)

Not all of the kings were bad. For example:

Jehoshaphat was thirty-five years old when he became king, and he reigned in Jerusalem for twenty-five years. His mother's name was Azubah daughter of Shilhi. In everything he walked in the ways of his father Asa and did not stray from them*; he did what was right in the eyes of the LORD.* (1 Kings 22:42-43)

But why didn't the Lord bring about the judgments stated in Deuteronomy 28? Here, again, we see the character of God coming through; His patience and longsuffering, His mercy and forgiveness, His grace and love. What He did do was to send the prophets, the first of whom was Elijah, who appeared on the scene in

1 Kings 17 when Ahab was king of the northern kingdom.

The Prophets

A prophet was not primarily someone who proclaimed what was to happen in the future. A prophet was a mouthpiece of God and, as such, may say what God has done in the past, or what He is doing in the present, or what He will do in the future. Often the 'future' prediction was dependent. For example, if the people repented then they would be blessed, but if they did not, there was the threat of judgment.

The prophets were sent primarily to the kings and leaders, telling them of the evil they had done and how they were not obeying the Law of Moses. For example:

> Then the word of the LORD came to Elijah the Tishbite: "Go down to meet Ahab king of Israel, who rules in Samaria. He is now in Naboth's vineyard, where he has gone to take possession of it. Say to him, 'This is what the LORD says: Have you not murdered a man and seized his property?'

Then say to him, 'This is what the LORD says: In the place where dogs licked up Naboth's blood, dogs will lick up your blood - yes, yours!'"

Ahab said to Elijah, "So you have found me, my enemy!" "I have found you," he answered, "because *you have sold yourself to do evil in the eyes of the LORD.* 'I am going to bring disaster on you.'" (1 Kings 21:17-21; see also, for example, 10:31; 14:4; 17:34)

The prophets were effectively exhorting the leaders to return to the Law (e.g. 2 Kings 17:13,37; 21:8). Often they spoke of the threat of judgment, and sometimes picked up the themes of Deuteronomy 28. For example, compare the following:

Deuteronomy 28:18: The fruit of your womb will be cursed, and the crops of your land, and the calves of your herds and the lambs of your flocks.

This is alluded to by both Hosea and Jeremiah.

Hosea 9:11,16-17: "Ephraim's glory will fly away like a bird—no birth, no pregnancy, no conception ... Ephraim is blighted, their root is withered, they yield no fruit. Even if they bear children, I will slay their cherished offspring." My God will reject them because they have not obeyed him; they will be wanderers among the nations.

Jeremiah 7:18-20: "The children gather wood, the fathers light the fire, and the women knead the dough and make cakes of bread for the Queen of Heaven. They pour out drink offerings to other gods to provoke me to anger. But am I the one they are provoking? declares the LORD. Are they not rather harming themselves, to their own shame? Therefore this is what the Sovereign LORD says: My anger and my wrath will be poured out on this place, on man and beast, on the trees of the field and on the fruit of the ground, and it will burn and not be quenched."

Then we have Deuteronomy 28:19 which states:

> You will be cursed when you come in and cursed when you go out.

Isaiah alludes to this when he prophesied the fall of Sennacharib.

> "But I know where you stay and when you come and go and how you rage against me. Because you rage against me and your insolence has reached my ears, I will put my hook in your nose and my bit in your mouth, and I will make you return by the way you came." (2 Kings 19:27)

In Deuteronomy 28:20 we have:

> The LORD will send on you curses, confusion and rebuke in everything you put your hand to, until you are destroyed and come to sudden ruin because of the evil you have done in forsaking him.

"Curses" in the Hebrew is *me'elah* and this word occurs in Jeremiah 29:18; 42:18; 44:12; Daniel 9:11 and Zechariah 5:3. "Confusion" is *mehumah* and is often translated 'turmoil' and it occurs in 2 Chronicles 15:5; Ezekiel 7:7; 22:5; Amos 3:9. The verbal form of "rebuke" occurs in Isaiah 30:17; 50:2. "Destroy" and / or "perish" occur in Jeremiah 27:10,15; Amos 9:8; Ezekiel 25:7.

In Deuteronomy 28:21 we read:

> The LORD will plague you with diseases until he has destroyed you from the land you are entering to possess.

The word for "disease", *dever*, occurs 17 times in Jeremiah and 11 times in Ezekiel and elsewhere in the prophets.

All this, and more, shows just how much the warnings of the prophets were in harmony with Deuteronomy 28. However, by and large the majority of the kings ignored the prophets, and failed to implement the Law of Moses, and it is doubtful if many ever made their own copy. It seems that some never even saw a copy because at one time, the Law was lost. However, when King Josiah of Judah was 26 we read:

> Hilkiah the high priest said to Shaphan the secretary, "I have found the Book of the Law in the temple of the LORD." He gave it to Shaphan, who read it. Then Shaphan the secretary went to the king and reported to him: "Your officials have paid out the money that was in the temple of the LORD and have entrusted it to the workers and supervisors at the temple." Then Shaphan the secretary informed the king, "Hilkiah the priest has given me a book." And Shaphan read from it in the presence of the king.
>
> When the king heard the words of the Book of the Law, he tore his robes. He gave these orders to Hilkiah the priest, Ahikam son of Shaphan, Acbor son of Micaiah, Shaphan the secretary and Asaiah the king's attendant: "Go and inquire of the LORD for me and for the people and for all Judah about what is written in this book

that has been found. Great is the LORD's anger that burns against us because our fathers have not obeyed the words of this book; they have not acted in accordance with all that is written there concerning us." (2 Kings 22:8-13)

Judgment fell

However, many years before King Josiah reigned over the southern kingdom of Judah, the northern kingdom of Israel had a succession of kings who "did evil in the sight of the Lord", namely Zachariah, Shallum, Menahem, Pekahiah, Pekah and Hoshea. Prophets like Amos and Hosea were sent but not listened to. The result of this was that the judgment of Deuteronomy 28, particularly verses 49-52, fell, and the northern kingdom was conquered and exiled to Assyria.

In the twelfth year of Ahaz king of Judah, Hoshea son of Elah became king of Israel in Samaria, and he reigned for nine years. He did evil in the eyes of the LORD, but not like the kings of Israel who preceded him. Shalmaneser king of Assyria came up to attack Hoshea ... Shalmaneser seized him and put him in prison.

The king of Assyria invaded the entire land, marched against Samaria and laid siege to it for three years. In the ninth year of Hoshea, the king of Assyria captured Samaria and deported the Israelites to Assyria. He settled them in Halah, in Gozan on the Habor River and in the towns of the Medes.

All this took place because the Israelites had sinned against the LORD their God, who had brought them up out of Egypt from under the power of Pharaoh king of Egypt. They worshipped other gods and followed the practices of the nations the LORD had driven out before them, as well as the practices that the kings of Israel had introduced.(2 Kings 17:1-8)

Seeing what was happening to Israel, one would have thought that the southern kingdom, Judah, would have certainly kept in line. However, King Ahaz of Judah did not do what was right in the eyes of the Lord (2 Kings 16:2) and Isaiah the prophet was sent to exhort a return to the duties specified in the Law of Moses; e.g. "Seek justice, encourage the oppressed. Defend the cause of the fatherless, plead the case of the widow," (Isaiah 1:17).. Just as the northern kingdom, Israel, was about to be taken into captivity (or had already been taken into captivity) so this could happen to Judah. Isaiah was sent to warn them of the danger of judgment.

> He said, "Go and tell this people: `Be ever hearing, but never understanding; be ever seeing, but never perceiving.' Make the heart of this people calloused; make their ears dull and close their eyes. Otherwise they might see with their eyes, hear with their ears, understand with their hearts, and turn and be healed."
>
> Then I said, "For how long, O Lord?" And he answered: "Until the cities lie ruined and without inhabitant, until the houses are left deserted and the fields ruined and ravaged, until the LORD has

sent everyone far away and the land is utterly forsaken." (Isaiah 6:9-12)

Hezekiah was the next king, and he did right in the eyes of the Lord (2 Kings 18:1-3), but in the end Judah also suffered from a succession of kings who did evil in the eyes of the Lord: Jehoahaz, Jehoiakim, Jehoiachin and Zedekiah. They did not heed the prophets that God sent, including Jeremiah.

> The word came to Jeremiah concerning all the people of Judah in the fourth year of Jehoiakim son of Josiah king of Judah, which was the first year of Nebuchadnezzar king of Babylon. So Jeremiah the prophet said to all the people of Judah and to all those living in Jerusalem: "For twenty-three years - from the thirteenth year of Josiah son of Amon king of Judah until this very day - *the word of the LORD has come to me and I have spoken to you again and again, **but you have not listened**. And though the LORD has sent all his servants the prophets to you*

again and again, **you have not listened or paid any attention**." They said, "Turn now, each of you, from your evil ways and your evil practices, and you can stay in the land the LORD gave to you and your fathers for ever and ever. Do not follow other gods to serve and worship them; do not provoke me to anger with what your hands have made. Then I will not harm you."

"But you did not listen to me," declares the LORD, "and you have provoked me with what your hands have made, and you have brought harm to yourselves."

Therefore the LORD Almighty says this: "Because you have not listened to my words, I will summon all the peoples of the north and my servant Nebuchadnezzar king of Babylon," declares the LORD, "and I will bring them against this land and its inhabitants and against all the surrounding nations. I will completely destroy them and make them an object of horror and scorn, and an everlasting ruin. I will banish from them the sounds of joy and gladness, the voices of bride and bridegroom, the sound of millstones and the light of the lamp. This whole country will become a desolate wasteland, and these nations will serve the king of Babylon seventy years. (Jeremiah 25:1-11)

In spite of the dire prophecy from Jeremiah, in spite of what had happened to the northern kingdom, did the southern kingdom, Judah, do as Jeremiah pleaded? Did they "turn now, each of you from your evil ways and evil practices"? Did they "stay the hand of the Lord"? Amazingly the answer is 'No!'

The LORD, the God of their fathers, sent word to them through his messengers again and again, because he had pity on his people and on his dwelling place. But they mocked God's messengers, despised his words and scoffed at his prophets until the wrath of the LORD was aroused against his people and there was no remedy.

He brought up against them the king of the Babylonians, who killed their young men with the sword in the sanctuary, and spared neither young man nor young woman, old man or aged. God handed all of them over to Nebuchadnezzar. He carried to Babylon all the articles from the temple of God, both large and small, and the treasures of the LORD's temple and the treasures of the king and his officials. They set fire to God's temple and broke down the wall of Jerusalem; they burned all the palaces and destroyed everything of value there. He carried into exile to Babylon the remnant who escaped from the sword, and they became servants to him and his sons until the kingdom of Persia came to power.

The land enjoyed its sabbath rests; all the time of its desolation it rested, until the seventy years were completed in fulfilment of the word of the LORD spoken by Jeremiah. (2 Chronicles 36:15-21)

And after seventy years the king of Persia allowed them to return to their land, to rebuild Jerusalem and the temple ... and to await their Messiah.

The New Testament

Some of what our Lord Jesus Christ taught was based upon Deuteronomy 28. For example: consider Matthew 6:25-33, where Christ said:

"Therefore I tell you, do not worry about your life, what you will eat or drink; or about your body, what you will wear. Is not life more important than food, and the body more important than clothes? Look at the birds of the air; they do not sow or reap or store away in barns, and yet your heavenly Father feeds them. Are you not much more valuable than they? Who of you by worrying can add a single hour to his life?

"And why do you worry about clothes? See how the lilies of the field grow. They do not labour or spin. Yet I tell you that not even Solomon in all his splendour was dressed like one of these. If that is how God clothes the grass of the field, which is here today and tomorrow is thrown into the fire, will he not much more clothe you, O you of little faith?

So do not worry, saying, `What shall we eat?' or `What shall we drink?' or `What shall we wear?' For the pagans (Gentiles, *KJV*) run after all these things, and your heavenly Father knows that you need them.

But seek first his kingdom and his righteousness, and all these things will be given to you as well.

The "all things" are, from the context, some of the main blessings of Deuteronomy 28; food, drink and clothing. These they would have if, under the terms of Deuteronomy 28, they carefully followed God's commands or, in the words of Christ, if they sought first God's kingdom and righteousness. Christ clearly demonstrated this by miraculously feeding them, five thousand on one occasion and four thousand on another, and there may well have been others which are not recorded.

There should be no chapter break here and our Lord went on to tell them:

> "Ask and it will be given to you; seek and you will find; knock and the door will be opened to you. For everyone who asks receives; he who seeks finds; and to him who knocks, the door will be opened.
>
> Which of you, if his son asks for bread, will give him a stone? Or if he asks for a fish, will give him a snake? If you, then, though you are evil, know how to give good gifts to your children, how much more will your Father in heaven give good gifts to those who ask him!
>
> So in everything, do to others what you would have them do to you, for this sums up the Law and the Prophets." (Matthew 7:7-12)

So what sort of things could they ask for and expect to receive? The prior context (Matthew 6:31-34) and the following context (Matthew 7:9) is to do with food, and these are the "good gifts" they could expect from God, all in terms with the Law, which Christ mentioned in verse 12. In the similar passage in Luke 11:11-13 Christ mentions "eggs" but also expanded the promise to include the Holy Spirit.

Israel were still, at that time, the Nation that God was dealing with and were told "Do not give dogs what is sacred; do not throw your pearls to pigs" (Matthew 7:6). "Dogs" and "pigs" were derogatory expressions used of Gentiles, and when Christ sent his disciples out He did so with specific instructions to go only to Israel, and not to the Gentiles.

> These twelve Jesus sent out with the following instructions: "Do not go among the Gentiles or enter any town of the Samaritans. Go rather to the lost sheep of Israel." (Matthew 10:5-6)

And He, Himself, said, He had been sent only to Israel (Matthew 15:24).

> A Canaanite woman from that vicinity came to him, crying out, "Lord, Son of

David, have mercy on me! My daughter is suffering terribly from demon-possession." Jesus did not answer a word. So his disciples came to him and urged him, "Send her away, for she keeps crying out after us." He answered, "I was sent only to the lost sheep of Israel." (Matthew 15:22-24)

Jesus was proclaimed as Israel's Messiah and He taught them, but His teaching was opposed by the leaders who, ultimately, rejected Him personally and crucified Him. The chief priests and the Sanhedrin of leaders influenced the crowds who joined in shouting, "Crucify him! Crucify him!" and such was their fury against Him that they cried out, "Let his blood be on us and on our children" (Matthew 27:22-25).

The sin of ignorance

However, on the cross our Saviour prayed, "Father, forgive them, for they do not know what they are doing" (Luke 23:34). This was echoed by Peter, when he addressed the Jews in Jerusalem a little while later:

"Men of Israel, why does this surprise you? Why do you stare at us as if by our own power or godliness we had made this man walk? The God of Abraham, Isaac and Jacob, the God of our fathers, has glorified his servant Jesus. You handed him over to be killed, and you disowned him before Pilate, though he had decided to let him go. You disowned the Holy and Righteous One and asked that a murderer be released to you. You killed the author of life, but God raised him from the dead. We are witnesses of this. By faith in the name of Jesus, this man whom you see and know was made strong. It is Jesus' name and the faith that comes through him that has given this complete healing to him, as you can all see. Now, brothers, I know that *you acted in ignorance*, as did your leaders. (Acts 3:12-17)

It appears then that both the people and their leaders – the high-priests and the Sanhedrin – acted in ignorance when they crucified Jesus. They were unaware that they were crucifying the

Christ, their Messiah, the Son of God. It was an unintentional sin and under the terms of Leviticus 4:13-15 they could be forgiven provided the leaders made the right sacrifice. Well here The Leader, Jesus, made The Sacrifice, and His prayer was, indeed, answered. But why were the people of that time unaware of the fact that Jesus was the Christ? How were they ignorant of the truth that He was their Messiah?

The Messiah in the Old Testament

In the Old Testament, there seems to be two pictures of the Messiah. One is termed the *Messiah-ben-David* and the other *Messiah-ben-Joseph*. The first refers to Him coming with power and great glory, a great King who is to set up His kingdom upon the earth, just as David was the conquering King of Israel. The second pictures Him as a suffering Messiah, lowly and rejected, just as Joseph was rejected by his brothers and sold for 30 pieces of silver. The Old Testament was the only Scriptures the Jews of the first century had, and they found it hard, even impossible, to marry these two descriptions of the Messiah. They had been under the domination of the Romans, and other powers, for centuries and so it was natural that they longed for and looked for the *Messiah-ben-David*. They wanted a great and glorious king who would free their land of the Romans and, instead, set up a righteous kingdom with themselves, the Jews, being the dominant nation, as opposed to being surfs.

For us, living after the events and with a completed Bible, we can see that the two descriptions of the Messiah refer to Christ's first and second comings. However, the Jews of the first century were not in such a fortunate position. Thus their sociological situation (an occupied nation), their desire (for a king to free them) and the theological teaching of their day (which either ignored the teachings of the suffering Messiah or applied such teaching to themselves, the Nation) blinded them as to who Jesus was. Thus they acted in ignorance and were unaware as to just who Jesus was. As such they could be forgiven and so Peter called upon those people to repent.

Repent, then, and turn to God, so that your sins may be wiped out, that times of refreshing may come from the Lord, and that he may send the Christ, who has been appointed for you - even Jesus. He must remain in heaven until the time comes for God to restore everything, as he promised long ago through his holy prophets. (Acts 3:19-21)

So if the people, particularly the leaders, repented then ...

- Their sins would be wiped out,
- The times of refreshing would come,
- And Christ would return.

How very similar to the call of the prophets of the Old Testament, but did the Jewish leadership who had crucified Christ repent? As we read through the Acts we see the opposition continued from the leaders. For example:

- Peter and John were imprisoned by the high-priest and opposed by the Sadducees, the rulers, elders and teachers of the Law; Acts 4:1,3-6.

- The high-priest gave Saul of Tarsus letters to enable him to imprison Jews who believed Jesus to be their Messiah; Acts 9:1-2.
- King Herod had the Apostle James beheaded and imprisoned Peter; Acts 12:1-5.
- They plotted to kill Paul, so much so that an army escorted him from Jerusalem to Caesarea; Acts 23:12,23-24.

For thirty or more years after the resurrection God sent apostles and prophets to the people of Israel, exhorting them to repent and turn to believe that Jesus was the Christ (Messiah), the Son of God, their Saviour. But just as in Jeremiah's day, they did not listen to the messengers. At the end of Acts we have two significant events. One is recorded in Josephus.

But this younger Ananus, who, as we have already told you took the high-priesthood, was a bold man in his temper, and very insolent; he was also of the sect of the Sadducees, who were very rigid in judging offenders, above all the rest of the Jews, as we have already observed; when, therefore, Ananus was of this disposition, he thought he had now a proper opportunity [to exercise his authority]. Festus was now dead, and Albinus was but upon the road; so he assembled the Sanhedrin of judges and brought before them the brother of Jesus, who was called the Christ, whose name was James, and some others, [or some of his companions;] and when he had formed an accusation against them as breakers of the law, he delivered them to be stoned; but as for those who seemed the most equitable of the citizens, and such as were the most uneasy at the breach of the laws, they disliked what was done; they also sent to the king [Agrippa], desiring him to send to Ananus that he should act so no more, for that what had already been done was not to be justified' nay, some of them went also to meet Albinus, as he was upon his journey from Alexandria, and informed him that it was not lawful for Ananus to assemble a Sanhedrin without his consent: whereupon Albinus complied with what they had said and wrote in anger to Ananus, and threatened that he would bring him to punishment for what he had done; on which king Agrippa took the highpriesthood from him, when he had ruled but three months, and made Jesus, the son of Damneus, high priest. (Josephus, *Antiquities of the Jews*, 20, 9, 1)

So hostile were the Jewish leadership towards Christianity that they stoned James, who was the leader of the church in Jerusalem, and other leading Christians which, according to one tradition, included the Apostle John: (and this tradition of the martyrdom of John is in harmony with Scripture: see Mark 10:38-40).

We read of Festus and King Agrippa in Acts chapters 25-26, when Paul appeared before them. Festus was procurator of Judea for only about two years (AD 60-62) when he suddenly died. Albinus was appointed in his place and it seems that during the hiatus in the governorship the high priest Ananus saw his opportunity. While Albinus was on the road from Alexandria to take up his appointment, Ananus had James, and other Christian leaders, stoned to death. This was against Roman law and just as the Sanhedrin had condemned Christ, but could not put Him to death without the approbation of the Roman procurator, neither could Ananus and his Sanhedrin put James and his companions to death without permission from Albinus.

However, all this enables us to place the martyrdom of James soon after the death of Festus. In other words James and the other Christian leaders in Jerusalem were stoned to death in AD 62. This was about the time Paul arrived in Rome and called together the leaders of the Jews, and this is the second significant event.

In the Acts we read of Paul's journeys and everywhere he went he always went first to the people of Israel, to the synagogue of the Jews. They still had first place in God's plan and, according, to Romans, which was written during the time covered by the Acts of the Apostles, they had certain privileges.

> I am not ashamed of the gospel, because it is the power of God for the salvation of everyone who believes: first for the Jew, then for the Gentile. (Romans 1:16)

And we see Paul doing this on his travels, always going to the synagogues and the Jewish people first, and this is what he told the Jews in Antioch.

> When the Jews saw the crowds, they were filled with jealousy and talked abusively against what Paul was saying. Then Paul and Barnabas answered them boldly: *"We had to speak the word of God to you first. Since you reject it and do not consider yourselves worthy of eternal life, we now turn to the Gentiles."* (Acts 13:45-46)

So, at that time, the gospel had to be preached to the Jew first, and there were other things where the Jew had a prior position.

There will be trouble and distress for every human being who does evil: first for the Jew, then for the Gentile; but glory, honour and peace for everyone who does good: first for the Jew, then for the Gentile. (Romans 2:9-10)

Israel did have truly wonderful blessings during the Acts period, far more than the Gentiles experienced, but they also experienced judgments; e.g. Ananias and Sapphira were struck dead (Acts 5:1-10); King Herod was struck dead (Acts 12:19-23 and see also Josephus *Antiquities of the Jews* 19,8,2 which describes this amazing event in detail); Elymas was struck blind (Acts 13:8-11). We read of no such judgments upon the Gentiles. Also a famine afflicted the area and Judea suffered badly (Acts 11:28-29). Thus God's judgments, under the terms of Deuteronomy 28, were beginning to fall.

However, Paul arrived in Rome more or less at the same time James was being stoned to death in Jerusalem. In Rome Paul called the leaders of the Jews together and tried to persuade them that

Jesus was the Christ, the Son of God. However, he met with the same reaction as in other places. Some of the Jew believed and some did not (Acts 28:17-24). By this time God's patience had run out and so Paul quoted Isaiah 6 against them again, and this is the last time this judgmental prophecy is quoted chronologically in the New Testament.

> They disagreed among themselves and began to leave after Paul had made this final statement: "The Holy Spirit spoke the truth to your forefathers when he said through Isaiah the prophet:
> 'Go to this people and say, "You will be ever hearing but never understanding; you will be ever seeing but never perceiving." For this people's heart has become calloused; they hardly hear with their ears, and they have closed their eyes. Otherwise they might see with their eyes, hear with their ears, understand with their hearts and turn, and I would heal them.'"
> (Act 28:25-27)

It seems the Jews had so hardened their hearts against the message that Jesus was the Christ that they no longer saw the significance of the miraculous signs, and no longer listened to what the Apostles taught concerning Him and to the theological arguments they put forward to support their case.

Christ had quoted from Isaiah 6 on a number of occasions when on earth, warning the people of Israel of possible judgment (e.g. Matthew 13:13-15; John 12:39-40), and Paul had also quoted it earlier (see Romans 11:7-8).

Here, at the end of Acts – following the stoning of James and the other Christians in Jerusalem and following the disagreement amongst the Jewish leaders in Rome – we have the final pronouncement of Isaiah 6. That being the case, we should expect some severe judgment to fall upon Israel, and it did.

In less than ten years the Romans destroyed Jerusalem and the Temple, massacred many of the Jews and exiled the rest throughout the

Roman Empire. Just as centuries earlier the northern kingdom had been exiled by the Assyrians, and the southern kingdom by the Babylonians, so those Jews who had rejected Jesus in person and who failed to repent at the call of the Apostles ... they were exiled by the Romans.

The Judgment and then Acts 28:28

After quoting from Isaiah 6 Paul made a significant statement. He said:

> "Therefore I want you to know that God's salvation has been sent to the Gentiles, and they will listen!" (Acts 28:28)

Within a couple of years of writing this he wrote to the Colossians, and there he stated:

> My fellow prisoner Aristarchus sends you his greetings, as does Mark, the cousin of Barnabas. (You have received instructions about him; if he comes to you, welcome him.) Jesus, who is called Justus, also

sends greetings. *These are the only Jews* among my fellow workers for the kingdom of God, and they have proved a comfort to me. (Colossians 4:10-11)

This hardness of heart by the Jews continued and following their exile by the Romans in AD 70. When early church history opens in the second century AD, all of the early Church Fathers were Gentiles. There was not one Jew amongst them! God's salvation had, indeed, been sent to the Gentiles. Deuteronomy 28 had again been fulfilled.

Appendix 1:

What happened after the end of Acts?

We concluded our study of Deuteronomy 28 by mentioning that all the early Church Fathers were Gentiles and that soon after Acts 28:28, Paul stated that the only Jews among his workers were Aristarchus, Mark and Justus. In fact the change which came about following the last pronouncement of Isaiah 6 in Acts 28:25-27 was swift and significant, as we can see from an analysis of the New Testament, which can be split into three time frames.

- The Gospel Period
- The Acts Period
- The Post Acts Period

Certain documents are associated with each of these periods.

The Gospel Period

The books associated with this period are, obviously, Matthew, Mark, Luke, John.

The Acts Period

There are two groups of letters associated with this period.

- (a) Letters written to Christian Jews, generally of the dispersion.
  Hebrews, James, 1 & 2 Peter, 1 & 2 & 3 John, Jude, Revelation
- (b) Letters Paul wrote to Jewish and Gentile Christians in various churches
  Romans, 1 & 2 Corinthians, Galatians, 1 & 2 Thessalonians

The Post Acts Period

These are the letters Paul wrote after the final pronouncement of Isaiah 6 in Acts 28:25-27 and his statement in Acts 28:28 that God's salvation had been sent to the Gentiles. These were Ephesians, Philippians, Colossians, 1 & 2 Timothy, Titus, Philemon.

When we analyse the New Testament in this way, we will note some interesting features. For example, consider how many times the following six words occur:

	Gospels	Acts	Acts Period Letters to Jews	Acts Period Letters to Jews & Gentiles	Post Acts Letters
Abraham	34	7	13	19	0
Isaac	8	4	5	3	0
Jacob	14	8	3	2	0
Moses	38	19	13	9	1
Jew(s)	88	82	2	27	1
Covenant(s)	9	2	18	8	1
Total	**191**	**122**	**54**	**68**	**3**

These figures are taken from Wigram's *Englishman's Greek Concordance of the New Testament* and the totals for the three time periods of the New Testament are:

Total for the Gospel Period: 191
Total for the Acts Period: 244
Total for Post Acts Period: 3

It is, perhaps, surprising that there is not even one mention of any of the big three (Abraham, Isaac and Jacob) in any of the Post Acts letters, and Moses is mentioned in just one verse. There we read:

> Just as Jannes and Jambres opposed Moses, so also these men oppose the truth - men of depraved minds, who, as far as the faith is concerned, are rejected. (2 Timothy 3:8)

Here Moses is not mentioned to give authority or back up something Paul was writing, but Paul referred to an incident in Moses' life in which Moses was opposed, as Christians were being opposed in Paul's day.

Similarly there is only one reference to 'Jew'. That is in Colossians 3:11 where we read, "Here there is no Greek or Jew, circumcised or uncircumcised, barbarian, Scythian, slave or free, but Christ is all, and is in all." There is also one reference to 'Jewish'. In Titus 1:14 Paul wrote, "pay no attention to Jewish myths". Neither of these passages show any preference towards Israel.

Again, there is just one mention of the word 'covenant' in the Post Acts period.

> Therefore, remember that formerly you who are Gentiles by birth and called "uncircumcised" by those who call themselves "the circumcision" (that done in the body by the hands of men) - remember that at that time you were separate from Christ, excluded from citizenship in Israel and foreigners to the covenants of the promise, without hope and without God in the world. But now in Christ Jesus you who once were far away have been brought near through the blood of Christ. (Ephesians 2:11-13)

The lack of references to 'covenant' should not surprise us for Paul had earlier written that the covenants[1] belonged to Israel (Romans 9:4). Ephesians 2:11-13 indicates the change in status of the Gentiles, from being second to the Jews (as they were in the Acts Period) to being on an equality, and this is further demonstrated when we look at the only reference to 'Jew' after Acts 28:28.

> Here there is no Greek or Jew, circumcised or uncircumcised, barbarian, Scythian, slave or free, but Christ is all, and is in all. (Colossians 3:11)

This verse does not indicate that the premier place is held by the Jews, rather the reverse; that

---

[1] Some may think that the *New Covenant* is an exception to Romans 9:4. However, Jeremiah 31:31 and Hebrews 8:8 make it very clear that it is not an exception. There we read, "The time is coming ... when I shall make a new covenant with the house of *Israel* and the house of *Judah*." And Jeremiah 33:33 and Hebrews 8:10 emphasis this. (For more on the New Covenant, see Appendix 3.)

there is no significance in being a Jew any longer.

However, the type of analysis demonstrated in the table above can be applied to many other words (e.g. Israel, Hebrew) and subjects (e.g. Sabbath, healing) and the results are worthy of investigation. There really was a great shift in God's purposes at the end of Acts, away from the Nation of Israel and towards all nations. This was the point in time when Israel were temporarily set aside and when the Church, the Body of Christ, began.

The change

From Genesis 12:1-3 until the end of Acts Abraham and his descendents had the first place in God's dealings with mankind. Although many Christians accept this for the Old Testament, they are reluctant to do so for the New. However, as we have seen, Christ stated He was sent only to Israel and when He sent His disciples out, He told them not to go to the Gentiles, but only to

Israel (see Matthew 10:5-6; 15:24). Also when Paul wrote to the Romans, he stated:

> For I tell you that Christ has become a servant of the Jews on behalf of God's truth, to confirm the promises made to the patriarchs. (Romans 15:8; *NIV*)

> Now I say that Jesus Christ was a minister of the circumcision for the truth of God, to confirm the promises made unto the fathers. (Romans 15:8; *KJV*)

We have already seen that during the Acts period the Jews also had first place, the gospel had to be preached to the Jews first, and they also had both the blessings and the judgments first.

The Jews were first, and the Jews were different. What made them first and different was the Law of Moses. Even during the Acts period it was incumbent upon the Jewish Christians to keep the Law of Moses, and we see this clearly demonstrated in the Acts of the Apostles where they visited the Temple for the feasts, observed the Sabbath, kept Nazirite vows (Numbers 6), practised circumcision etc.

However, following the final pronouncement of Isaiah 6 in Acts 28:25-27, and the impending judgment upon the Nation of Israel, the situation for the Jewish Christian changed. One aspect of this change was that, for them, the Law of Moses was abolished. They no longer needed to keep all its rites and ceremonies. Consider these two passages, written shortly after Acts 28:28, during Paul's two year imprisonment recorded in Acts 28:30-31.

> For he himself is our peace, who has made the two one and has destroyed the barrier, the dividing wall of hostility, by abolishing in his flesh the law with its commandments and regulations. His purpose was to create in himself one new man out of the two, thus making peace, and in this one body to reconcile both of them to God through the cross, by which he put to death their hostility. (Ephesians 2:14-16)

He forgave us all our sins, having cancelled the written code, with its regulations, that was against us and that stood opposed to us; he took it away, nailing it to the cross. And having disarmed the powers and authorities, he made a public spectacle of them, triumphing over them by the cross. Therefore do not let anyone judge you by what you eat or drink, or with regard to a religious festival, a New Moon celebration or a Sabbath day. These are a shadow of the things that were to come; the reality, however, is found in Christ. (Colossians 2:13-17)

Thus the Law of Moses was abolished for Jewish Christians at the *end* of Acts, and we are wrong to read this back into the Acts Period. Some commentators do this and so state that people like Paul were being unfaithful when he circumcised Timothy or undertook a Nazerite vow, etc. However, in this those commentators are wrong. Quite simply, if the Jewish Christians of the Acts Period had given up circumcision and Sabbath keeping, they would have been ineffective witnesses to those Jews who had not yet come to believe in Jesus. The non-Christian Jews would have called any Jewish Christian who did not keep the Law of Moses a Gentile dog, and would have had nothing to do with him. Thus the Jewish Christian was not freed from the Law of Moses until the Nation was under judgment.

In the Ephesian passage above we read that God had made the two (the Jewish Christian and the Gentile Christian) one, and this is emphasised in the next chapter of Ephesians.

> This mystery is that through the gospel the Gentiles are heirs together with Israel, members together of one body, and sharers together in the promise in Christ Jesus. (Ephesians 3:6)

Here, in the Greek, there is a threefold emphasis on equality. We could paraphrase that passage.

The Gentiles are co-heirs, co-members together in one body, and co-sharers in the promise in Christ Jesus.

Or:

The Gentiles are equal heirs, equal members together in one body, and equal sharers in the promise in Christ Jesus.

All this indicates that even before the destruction of Jerusalem by the Romans in AD 70, God had dismissed Israel. Those within Israel who believed in Christ were now one with the Gentiles who believed in Christ and they both had all the blessings of being a Christian ... but none of the previous blessings which belonged to the Nation of Israel and which we read of in Deuteronomy 28.

The blessings of Deuteronomy were for Israel and were 'earthly' blessings, to do with food and drink, clothing and health, protection from enemies and being the premier nation upon the earth. However, Ephesians does not speak of 'earthly' blessings but of 'spiritual' blessings, and these blessings are not upon this earth but are in the 'heavenly realms'.

> Praise be to the God and Father of our Lord Jesus Christ, who has blessed us in the heavenly realms with every spiritual blessing in Christ. (Ephesians 1:3)

> And God raised us up with Christ and seated us with him in the heavenly realms in Christ Jesus, in order that in the coming ages he might show the incomparable riches of his grace, expressed in his kindness to us in Christ Jesus. (Ephesians 2:6-7)

These are the blessings for this age of grace in which we live, and this is the hope for Christians in this present dispensation.

Appendix 2: Deuteronomy 28 and Josephus

Readers who possess a copy of *The Works of Josephus* will find *The Wars of the Jews* very relevant to the years from Acts 28:28 to AD 70.

Much of Deuteronomy 28 was supremely fulfilled in AD 70 and in the years preceding that calamity. There is a great deal of relevant material in *The Wars of the Jews*. Josephus gives much information concerning the wickedness of the Nation of Israel at that time (AD 62-70) and he also supplies many details concerning the siege of Jerusalem and the suffering of the inhabitants, illustrating some of the judgments mentioned in Deuteronomy 28:15-68.

Book 1 of *The Wars of the Jews* deals with the period from Antiochus Epiphanes to the death of Herod the Great. However, from chapter 14 of

Book 2, right through Books 3-7, there is much that is relevant to what happened to the Nation of Israel after they had been set aside by God at Acts 28:25-28.

The following are all taken from Book 5 of *The Wars of the Jews*. (The numbers refer to the chapter and paragraph.)

> **1.3.** An exclamation of Josephus, "O most wretched city, what misery so great as this didst thou suffer from the Romans, when they came to purify you from thy intestine hatred!"

> **10.5.** No city suffered such miseries, nor did any age breed a generation more fruitful in wickedness.

> **12:3.** Famine. (Deuteronomy 28:21)

These are taken from Book 6.

> **1.1.** The country itself desolate.

3.3. Famine. (Deuteronomy 28:21)

3.4. The eminent woman who ate her own son. (Deuteronomy 28:53-57)

4.5. The Temple burnt on 10th Ab, the same day as by Nebuchadnezzar. (Jeremiah 52:12-13)

5.3. Portents and wonders signifying doom.

8.2. A great number slain, but many more sold into slavery. But because there were so many, buyers were few. (Deuteronomy 28:68)

9.2. Many sent to Egyptian mines. (Deuteronomy 28:68)

9.3. The number of those taken captive 97,000. Those that perished 1,100,000.

And Book 7 records:

11.1. The city and temple destroyed except for three towers.

Appendix 3
The New Covenant

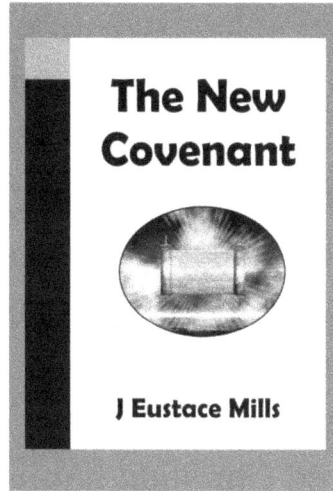

Details of these books can be seen on
www.obt.org.uk

The books can be ordered from that website and
from The Open Bible Trust Fordland Mount,
Upper Basildon, Reading, RG8 8LU, UK.

They are also available as eBooks
from Amazon and Apple
and as a KDP paperback from Amazon.

About the Author

Michael Penny was born in Ebbw Vale, Gwent, Wales in 1943. He read Mathematics at the University of Reading, before teaching for twelve years and becoming the Director of Mathematics and Business Studies at Queen Mary's College Basingstoke in Hampshire, England. In 1978 he entered Christian publishing, and in 1984 became the administrator of the Open Bible Trust.

He held this position for seven years, before moving to the USA and becoming pastor of Grace Church in New Berlin, Wisconsin. He returned to Britain in 1999, and is at present the Administrator and Editor of The Open Bible Trust.

From 2010 to 2018 he was Chairman of Churches Together in Reading, where he speaks in a number of churches, and was a chaplain at reading College and on the advisory committee to Reading University Christian Union.

He lives near Reading with his wife and has appeared on BBC Radio Berkshire and Premier Radio a number of times. He has made several speaking tours of America, Canada, Australia, New Zealand and the Netherlands, as well as ones to South Africa and the Philippines. Some of his writings have been translated into Russian.

As well as editing and writing articles for *Search* magazine and many Bible study booklets, he has also written several major books including: *The Manual on the Gospel of John; 40 Problem Passages; Approaching the Bible; Galatians - Interpretation and Application; The Miracles of the Apostles; Introducing God's Word* (with Carol Brown and Lynn Mrotek); *Introducing God's Plan* (with Sylvia Penny).

Recent books are *The Bible! Myth or Message?, The Balanced Christian Life* (based on Ephesians, and is designed for use with Lent Studies and House Group Bible Studies).

He has written two books with W M Henry

- *Following Philippians*, which is ideal for Post-Alpha groups
- *The Will of God: Past and Present.*

His latest books are:

- *Joel's Prophecy: Past and Future*
- *James; His Life and Letter*
- *Paul: A Missionary of Genius*
- *Peter: His life and letters*

Details of these books can be seen on
www.obt.org.uk

The books can be ordered from that website and from The Open Bible Trust Fordland Mount, Upper Basildon, Reading, RG8 8LU, UK.

They are also available as eBooks
from Amazon and Apple
and as a KDP paperback from Amazon.

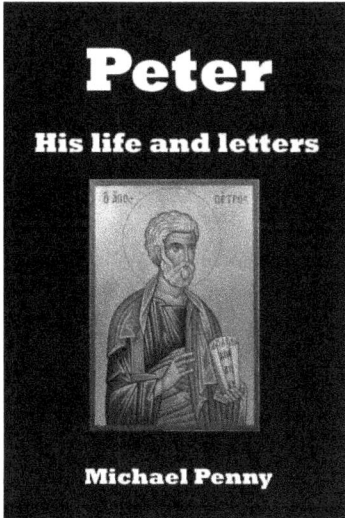

Peter
His life and letters

Michael Penny

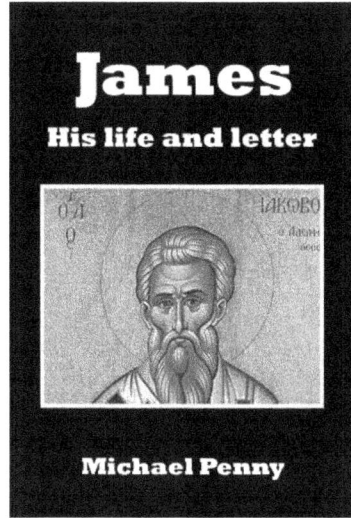

James
His life and letter

Michael Penny

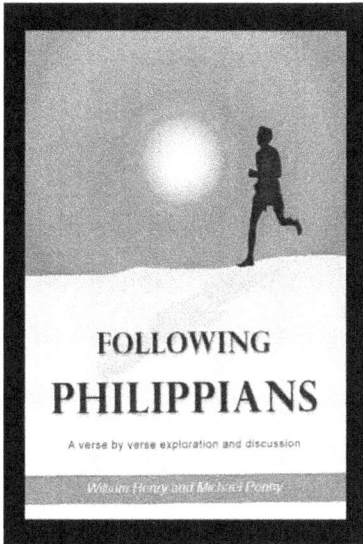

FOLLOWING
PHILIPPIANS

A verse by verse exploration and discussion

William Henry and Michael Penny

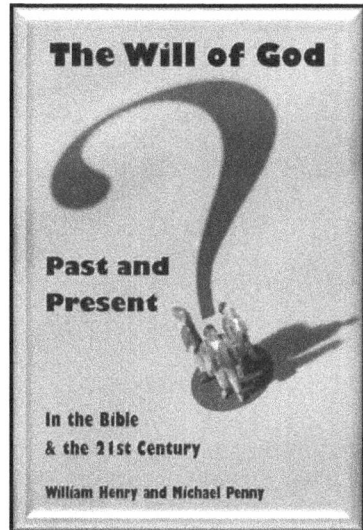

The Will of God

Past and Present

In the Bible
& the 21st Century

William Henry and Michael Penny

Also by Michael Penny

Approaching the Bible

Michael Penny

In easy to understand steps, this book sets out to encourage and stimulate Christians to approach the Bible for themselves. With many interesting examples, Michael Penny provides the rational for the view that before we try to *apply* any passage in the Bible to ourselves, we should discover first what it meant to those to whom its words were initially addressed. The book advocates that this is best done by considering the passage under the following headings:

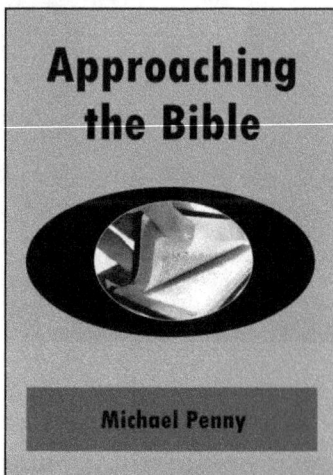

1) **W**ho said or wrote it;
2) to **W**hom was it said or written, or concerning **W**hom was it said or written;

3) **W**here it was said or written, or concerning **W**here was it said or written;

4) **W**hat was said or written;

5) **W**hen was it said or written, or concerning **W**hen was it said or written;

6) **W**hy was it said or written.

Applying these six **"W"** rules puts the passage into its proper context and gives us the right perspective on it. Only after doing this can we determine:

7) **W**hether the passage applies to our situation and what the correct application is.

It is the *consistent* use of these **Seven Ws** which helps us discover the right and relevant application of any passage to our lives.

****

Copies can be ordered from **www.obt.org.uk** and from The Open Bible Trust Fordland Mount, Upper Basildon, Reading, RG8 8LU, UK.

It is also available as an eBook from Amazon and Apple and as a KDP paperback from Amazon.

Free Magazine

Michael Penny is editor of *Search* magazine

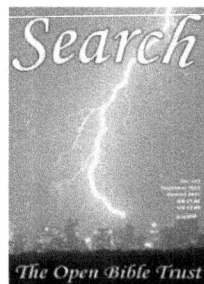

For a free sample of
the Open Bible Trust's magazine Search,
please visit

www.obt.org.uk/search

or email

admin@obt.org.uk

About this book

Deuteronomy 28
A key to understanding

Deuteronomy 28 is a chapter which is seldom referred to in commentaries and Christian literature, and probably never preached upon from the pulpit. Yet it is a key to understanding how God dealt with Israel in the Old Testament.

Not only that, it is essential to a right understanding of some of the things Christ said to the Jews when He was upon this earth, and to appreciating why certain events happened to that nation in the first century AD.

Publications of The Open Bible Trust must be in accordance with its evangelical, fundamental and dispensational basis. However, beyond this minimum, writers are free to express whatever beliefs they may have as their own understanding, provided that the aim in so doing is to further the object of The Open Bible Trust. A copy of the doctrinal basis is available on **www.obt.org.uk** or from:

THE OPEN BIBLE TRUST
Fordland Mount, Upper Basildon,
Reading, RG8 8LU, GB

www.ingramcontent.com/pod-product-compliance
Lightning Source LLC
Chambersburg PA
CBHW070543030426
42337CB00016B/2326